Dear Reader,

We all need our own little BLUEPRINTS, or plans, in life. Sometimes making a plan is fun. Sometimes it's hard. Sometimes the plan doesn't work, so we make a new one. And sometimes, the plan is exactly what we need, just when we need it. As you read this Have a Plan Book, we hope you will ask questions, talk about it with family and friends, and create your very own plan. You can do this on your own or together with a grown-up.

Your plan may grow and change each time you read your book, and that's great! As life happens, plans change. But remember, having a little Blueprint is always helpful, in difficult times and in good times. So go ahead: BLUEPRINT IT!

Lovingly,

Your friends at little BLUEPRINT

P.S. Children and adults around the world are making their own little BLUEPRINTS. If you want to see the plans of others, or share yours, just go to

www.littleBLUEPRINT.com

Jack-o-lantern

trick
or
treat

card

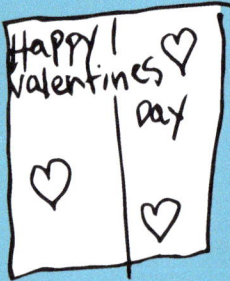

HAVE A PLAN Books

To purchase a hardcover or
personalized version of any
little BLUEPRINT book,
with names, optional photo(s),
and details, please go to:

www.littleBLUEPRINT.com

The author would like to thank,
for all of their support and expertise:
Dan Siegel, M.D.;
Nina Shapiro, M.D.; and
my editors, Leslie Budnick and Gina Shaw.
A special thanks to:
Phoebe, age 10, for her blueprint illustration; and
Brooke, age 10, for her title page illustration.

Boo

Turkey

Ba-Boom

fire works

A Day
of Thanks

Card

Happy Valentines Day

Be my valentine

Boo

Turkey

Ba-Boom

Fire works

Be my valentine

Ba-Boom

TO CELEBRATE
the Holidays,
I HAVE A PLAN

by Katherine Eskovitz

illustrated by Jessica Churchill

Fire works

Trick or Treat

Jack-o-lantern

I LOVE TO CELEBRATE

holidays!

A holiday is a day when we celebrate together
as **A FAMILY, A COMMUNITY, A NATION,**
or **A RELIGIOUS GROUP.**

Every holiday is special for its own reason.

HALLOWEEN is a community holiday when we have fun dressing up in costumes and going **TRICK OR TREATING** in our neighborhood.

THANKSGIVING is a national holiday when school is closed all across the country. We cook and eat a delicious meal together and talk about what we are thankful for in our lives.

VALENTINE'S DAY is a holiday that is celebrated in many countries.

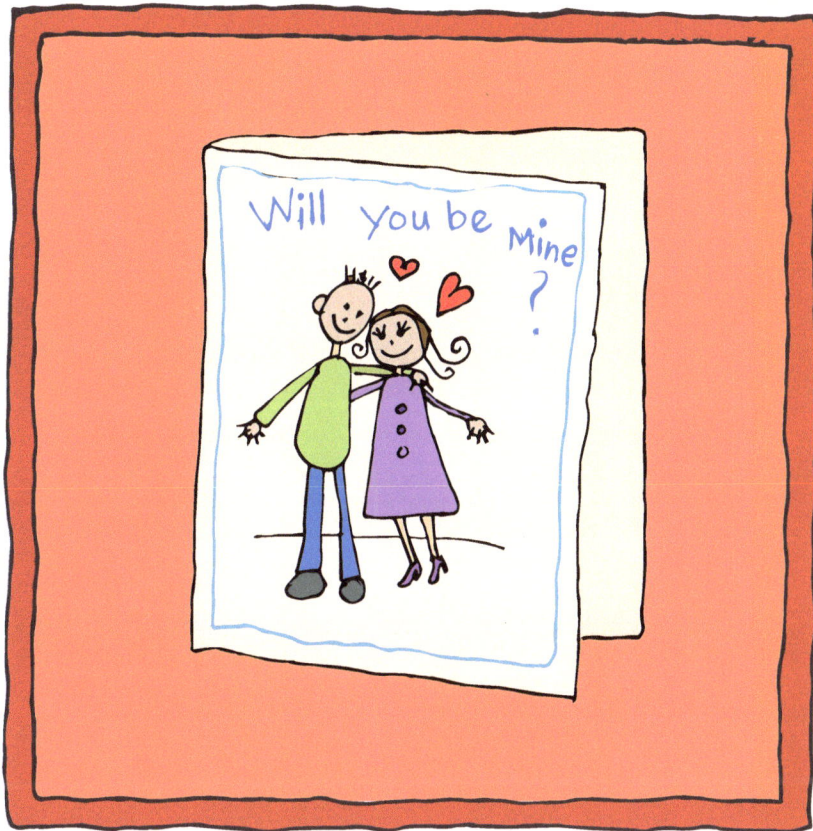

Will you be mine?

IT HAS BEEN A CELEBRATION OF LOVE

for people around the world for hundreds of years.

MY FAMILY CELEBRATES LOTS OF HOLIDAYS TOGETHER.

Every family has their own traditions and beliefs about HOLIDAYS.

I can talk with my parents about our family, what we celebrate throughout the year, and why.

HAPPY HOLIDAY

I can draw or paste
some of my
favorite holiday
celebrations here!

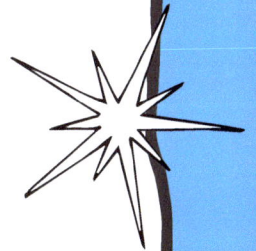

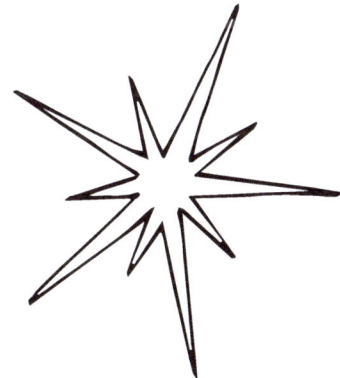

During the holidays,
our regular schedule often changes.

I may not have school or I may have a
celebration at school.

CLOSED
FOR THE
HOLIDAY

I might wear dressy clothes, visit family,
or stay up late to celebrate. YAY!

On some holidays, I get presents.

I love presents.

It is so much fun to open presents.

But holidays are about a lot more
than just presents.

Often, what we remember most about a holiday is the time we spend together, the thoughtful things we plan and do for each other, and our FAMILY TRADITIONS. These are the special things we do together, year after year, that are unique to our family and the holiday.

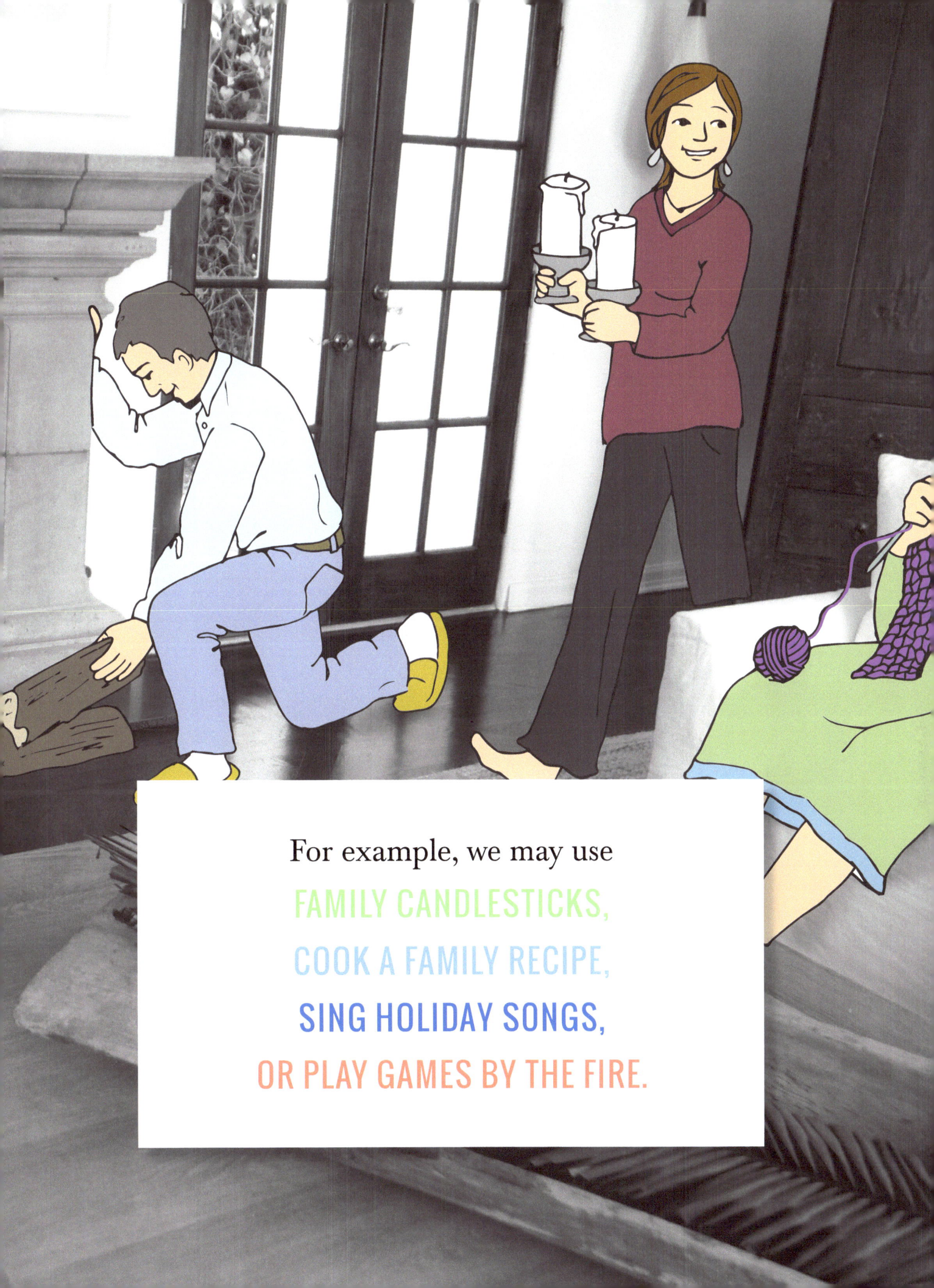

For example, we may use
FAMILY CANDLESTICKS,
COOK A FAMILY RECIPE,
SING HOLIDAY SONGS,
OR PLAY GAMES BY THE FIRE.

When we are preparing for a holiday,

I can help make it the most

MEMORABLE, SPECIAL, and FUN

celebration of that day

EVER!

I can make a special card showing what someone means to me,

write a poem, draw a picture, create a decoration…

anything to show how much I care.

I can make a list of everyone I want to honor for the holiday and think about what I could do for them.

I can be a DETECTIVE and write down CLUES about what friends and relatives might like by watching them and thinking about their interests.

I can make the day easier for someone I love

by making them breakfast in bed, setting the table,
cleaning up my room, or just by helping
with what needs to be done.

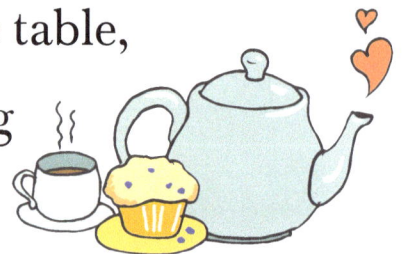

Instead of buying presents for each other, our family can give homemade gift certificates for fun activities. The holder could be entitled to a:

FAMILY PILLOW FIGHT,
PICNIC DINNER,
CAMPOUT IN THE BACKYARD,
TRIP FOR FROZEN YOGURT . . .

Ohhhh, it's exciting just thinking about the possibilities.

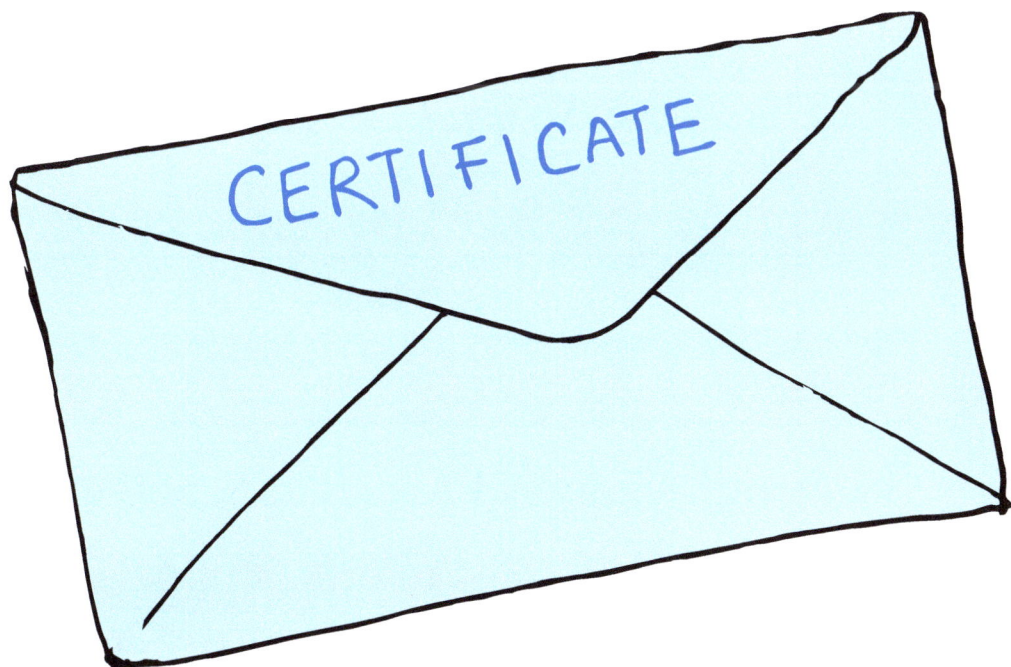

I can do something thoughtful
for someone I don't even know.

I can go through my toys, clothes, and games,

and donate items to others in need.

THAT WILL BRIGHTEN THEIR HOLIDAY.

I can raise money to give to a charity

by having a lemonade stand, a bake shop, a car wash...

THERE ARE SO MANY
FUN WAYS TO HELP OTHERS.

I can cook or bake with
my family for a holiday.

I can give our **HOME-BAKED TREATS** to my teachers
or others to let them know I appreciate them.

I can have a **DECORATING PARTY** with my family
and friends. We can make our own decorations so
that our house will look festive.

With the help of my family, I can create
new family traditions, too:

TRACING OUR HANDS ON THE TABLE
RUNNER EACH YEAR FOR THANKSGIVING,

COOKING OR BAKING NIGHT FOR
VALENTINE'S DAY,

TAKING A DRIVE IN OUR PAJAMAS TO SEE
HOLIDAY LIGHTS ON NEW YEAR'S EVE,

FAMILY GAME NIGHT ON
THE FOURTH OF JULY . . .

it can be anything at all!

I can start just by making my own plan

— along with my family —

of how to celebrate our next holiday in a special way.

I can't wait to celebrate!

Here is MY PLAN

Check out other children's BLUEPRINTS from around the world and share yours, too!

Other titles in the
HAVE A PLAN Series

TO BE A HEALTHY EATER, I HAVE A PLAN

WHEN IT'S TIME FOR BED, I HAVE A PLAN

WHEN I MISS SOMEONE SPECIAL, I HAVE A PLAN

WHEN I MISS MY SPECIAL PET, I HAVE A PLAN

TO BE SAFE AT HOME, I HAVE A PLAN

TO BE SAFE ON THE GO, I HAVE A PLAN

TO KEEP MY BODY SAFE, I HAVE A PLAN

WHEN MY PARENTS DIVORCE, I HAVE A PLAN

WHEN MY PARENTS SEPARATE, I HAVE A PLAN

AND MORE

New titles added regularly at

www.littleBLUEPRINT.com

All titles are available ready-made and personalized

little
BLUEPRINT
Empowering children. Training the brain.
WWW.LITTLEBLUEPRINT.COM